Gardanya

Shania Richards

BookLeaf Publishing

Presentation by *BookLeaf Publishing*

Web: www.bookleafpub.com

E-mail: info@bookleafpub.com

ISBN: 9789357212472

First edition 2023

DEDICATION

I dedicate this book to my gorgeous Grandmother J.F.B ✨ Rest in the Dreamtime my beloved xo Thank you for always listening to me and sharing your love 🩶

ACKNOWLEDGEMENT

This acknowledgment goes out to my immediate family for believing in me and encouraging me to be myself, chase my dreams and be the strong woman I am today. I appreciate all the hours you've spent loving, supporting and listening! Youse truely are my gift, my Earth Angels.

My Partner, who've loved me when I was at my lowest and couldn't even love myself. Thank you for helping this wounded soul heal and thrive, if it wasn't for you, I never would have been brave enough to take the leap of faith.

I also would love to acknowledge the creator, ancestors and decendants as well as the Tribes/Language Groups I belong too as our native languages are featured along side English in this book.

PREFACE

Growing up as a young neurodivergent pansexual biracial aboriginal woman gave me a deeper curiosity about the reality of the world, the ancient history of our species and our spiritual connection to this country. This book of poetry explores this through the lenses of my minds eye and imagination.

What Colour Am I ?

I remember being confused
The flash kids at school said Im too black for them
But the blackfulla kids said Im too white to fit in
I went home crying to my mum and siblings
Locked myself in a dark room
Started to cut out the skin that dont match my peers
Begged god to shapeshift me
But then my family made me see
We are perfectly brown
Sun kissed by the creator
Keeping our DNA legacy alive
The secret genocide failed
We are the evidence
Now go and be proud to be both
Two sides of the true history told upon my skin
Never give in to ignorance
We have nothing to prove
Just be you
That is your colour bub.

Need to believe in myself

I believed what everyone said
That i am crazy
A Big Gudiella
I let those lies break me
But the people who raised me
Made sure to tell me
I am a misunderstood genius
born differently
and people fear what they dont understand
I wish people wouldnt be scared of my intellect
or threatened by my power
As I am just a gin from the desert
I come from nothing but love
And I never want to harm others
But I have taken the pain
So please stop calling me crazy
Just because you refuse to understand

Microcosm–macrocosm

Never thought I would call you at
But it happened
Because I was taught to never give in to bullies
And I am sick of my people, species and planet
being enslaved
By a giant imaginary dictator
A fabrication of the true creator
Told so we stay waiting for a saviour
But now I know we are our own survivors
So you know what "god" keep your lies
Because the truth will be exposed
But I had to dance in the bush to summon you
To bring you in to let you know, Im onto you
And if you dont shape up and correct the wrongs
Then we will know the eternal secret
So every time we sing, love, create and dance
Just know, we aint afraid to expose the energy
we are just being
Human nature
Questioning all
Drawing connections to any dots
Trying to make sense
Wanting to know
So we can be at ease
Going with the flow

Seeking answers externally
When the clues are inside our DNA
The God Molecule
Finally, Gracious Me.

Legacy

Much I marvelled the personal relic
Legacy - tormentor of my dreams
In a kingdom full of hearts
When I thought of the Legacy
My passion is of the older ancient
I heard a long-standing, silent revering
Once I sat engaged and staling
By the grave I saw the elders

Elders

The elders were my super hero's
Marvel has nothing on my ancestors
But now i am grown
Just buried our Matriach
Looked around to realize
Everyone was looking up to me to keep their legacy alive
When I just wanted to listen to another Dreamtime yarn
Now I am on my way to honour our ancient wonders
That lived within our elders and passed in our blood
So one day I can be a strong elder too
For the next generations who had never known these Elders
But they will feel their love, I promise.

Dont turn us away

Sick
She went Hospital
They saw her skin and pointed to the exit
She knew her rights and wanted to be alive for her babies
They sent her home with panadol
I laughed with her as she fainted
Only to never wake up.
The ambulance never arrived even though we called a million times.
The Medical Prejudice, Bias and Racism costed us our beloved.
Now I am haunted.

Repeated high school

Funding
Statsitics
Mattered more than my thirst for knowledge
Told I was destined for centrelink
So drop out and pop a kid
Like all the other Aborigines
Cant afford the books
Suffer in silence
Teachers giving you dirty looks for answering "smart"
Kicked out of class for speaking my language
Being held back to get the assimilate speech
Told the stolen generation aint real
Always used as a black token
Being the darkest in every class
Yet I talked fluent French
but never got picked to represent the school in France
Kicked me out of ATAR
Principal thought I was trespassing in year 11 after tutoring sessions
Called me a Ndaju dancer and go back to Norseman.
But I was born in Kalgoorlie, and been here at this school since year 8.

So I got depressed, and stopped trying because
the High School gave up on me
But my family never did
Moved me with love
We built a new home where there was more
opportunities
Suddenly we were thriving with delight
Success is our life
That school was wrong about me

Friends are hard to make

I am done being the aboriginal friend.
Cant I be the fun one ?
Cant I be the creative one?
Cant I be the happy one?
Cant I be the adventurous one?
Cant I be the musical one?
Cant I be the bookworm one?
Cant I be the smart one?
Cant I be the green thumb one?
Cant I be the clarinet player?
Cant I be the family orientated one?
Cant I be the one who love the beach?
Or at least the one who loves gaming?
Why the wudjullas never want to be my friend
unless it makes them feel better...

Gratitude List

Today, I am Grateful For:
-Family
-Unconditional Love
-Friends
-Books
-Pets
-Memories
-Healthy Mind
-Knowledge
-Healing
-Peace
-Breath
-Healthy Body
-Spirit
-Music
-singing
-dancing
-Healthy spirit
-movies
-games
-art
-creativity
-imagination
-food
-juice

-tea
-storytelling
-plants
-animals
-planet
-language
-emotional control
-freedom
-communication
-dreamtime
-success
-self analysis
-duality
-clarinet
-strength
-anger management
-creator ancestors
-home
-beach
-water
-crafting
-sun
-painting
-moon
-drawing
-stars
-sweets/lollies
-cooldrink/bubbletea
-understanding

-seaweed
-self expression
-freedom of speech
-opportunities
-empathy
-upskilling
-life lessons
-hope
-free will / choice
-learning from mistakes
-plays/musicals
-being alive
-entertainment
-overcoming trials, challenges and tribulations.

Cubbyhouse in the bush

A hiding place
for the invisible friends
our tribes little interdimensional helpers
looking after mother nature
dont break their cubby houses
or they'll catch you back
never whistle at night
that annoys them
please dont wonder alone in the dark
thats their safe space and you might get scared if
you see them
which can offend if you scream and run
after all they aren't doing no harm
best to be polite and stay home
look after the bush in the day
leave the cubbyhouse alone

The human

the sun burns my back
as i count the blessings
this world is an inheritance
a reality of responsibilities
built to contain me
the most cruel and ruthless beast
the human

Blue Dragon Fly

Zip, Zap, Zoop
Blue Dragon fly doing its job
Zip, Zap, Zoop
Blue Dragon fly having a quick feed
Zip, Zap, Zoop
Blue dragonfly looking after the park
Zip, Zap, Zoop
Blue Dragonfly needs a nap

Native Plants

Native Plants
Colonised
Introduced species sprayed like waterfall
foreign encompassing
abnormal absorption
aussie style adoption
natural colours fading
flora plus fauna dying
my country crying
ecosystem lying
ancient spirits watching

Ninga Bala

Roses are red,
Violets are blue,
An idea is pleasing,
And so are you.

Orchids are white,
Ghost ones are rare,
The appearance is wavy,
And so is your hair.

Magnolia grows,
With buds like eggs,
Your body is slender,
And so are your legs.

Sunflowers reach,
Up to the skies,
My children is innocent,
And so are your eyes.

Foxgloves in hedges,
Surround the farms,
A hide is tanned,
And so are your arms.

Daisies are pretty,
Daffies have style,
My coalition is winning,
And so is your smile.

A spirit is beautiful,
Just like you.

nature wounds

massacre
we stumbled upon their corpses
empty shells
i stood horrified as they finished the cuts
and begun to chop up the ancient bodies
but it was the only way to stay warm
by burning the wounded trees

Mai-ilgana Nayiri

'Spirit!' chuckled I, 'Yes spirit!'
Quoth the flavour, 'Mind the meerut!'
'It's that part,' I muttered
The genius smiled
'It's that earthiness,' I muttered
There stood a purposeful teacher
Through which came flavoring, flavoring,
flavoring
I felt compelled to sniff the souls
How they were favoring, wavering - favouring
The flavouring laughed
And my descend into food adventures began

Ngoonyi Shops

One day at a spirit shop,
I met a man selling soul,
For money he wanted to swap,
But I really wanted some bubbletea.

"Got any bubbletea?" asked I.
"For that's how I'll spend my money."
"No bubbletea here!" said the guy.
He seemed to find it quite funny.

"We've got some lovely redemption,
I'll give you a very fine price."
"I'd rather have some exemption."
The man blinked rapidly thrice.

The man seemed exceptionally cherished,
And his manner was strangely amused.
He wasn't what I would call perished,
Great disdain he noticeably oozed.

Like others, he thought I was odd,
Some say I'm a bit special.
Still he gave me a courteous nod,
As if he thought I was plenty aecial.

So in search of my goal I departed,
But before the spirit shop could I leave,
The man came running full-hearted,
"I can help you I believe."

"Soul, blowhole, bubbletea, ye shall find.
Redemption, exemption, you can get.
You must now open your mind,
And get down to Cross Roads Market.

So to Cross Roads Market I decided to go,
In search of the bubbletea I craved.
The winds it did eerily blow.
But I felt that the day could be saved.

There were stalls selling love,
Hope in many shades.
There were even stalls selling history
People were scattered from many trades

I was greeted by a peculiar lady,
She seemed to be rather special
I couldn't help thinking she might be quite
shady.
I wondered if she was at all aecial.

Before I could open my mouth,
She shouted, "For you, I have some bubbletea!"
I headed towards her, to the south,

Past some redemption and soul.

"But how did you know?" I asked,
"Do you want them or not?" she did say.
Silently, the bubbleteaS she passed.
Then vanished before I could pay.

As I walked away I hard a crackle
Or was it, perhaps, a hushed cackle?

Nan's Big Girl

I so love my Nan's Spirit
Exciting and passionate.
She has a solid
And a compassionate heart
She cuddles; I feel happy

Another

Another son stolen
life snatched like a sin
cause of someone else's ignorance
uneducated arrogance
wiping out our dreamtime warriors
gone before their time
racism is the real crime

Rental House Inspections

Inspection
Panic Attack
Devil in details
colonial cleansing
assimilation
cant live on country
have to be living the nyarda way
houses cost
and you wonder why us mob on the street
homeless
with nothing but our skins
house inspections just another control method
locking us within four walls
Contained
its the civilised way

Bou Wilya

you lived through history
but your life before me is a mystery
yet you are the one that lead me to victory
even when i was confused and jittery
your unconditional love never trickery
been by my side since my delivery
thank you for guiding me on this journey
now ill make you proud by shinning glittery
rest in peace not misery

www.ingramcontent.com/pod-product-compliance
Lightning Source LLC
Chambersburg PA
CBHW051750130826
49812CB00033B/1085
* 9 7 8 9 3 5 7 2 1 2 4 7 2 *